21 Stories of Faith

Real People, Real Stories, Real Faith

Shelley Hitz
And Contributing Authors

21 Stories of Faith: Real People, Real Stories, Real Faith

Published by Body and Soul Publishing
Printed in the United States of America

ISBN-13: 978-0615989730
ISBN-10: 061598973X

Table of Contents

Introduction

By Shelley Hitz

"Now faith is the substance of things hoped for, the evidence of things not seen." ~ Hebrews 11:1 (NKJV)

Faith. What is the first thing that comes to your mind when you think of the word faith? I often think of faith as stepping out into the unknown, the evidence of things not seen, and ultimately giving up my control.

One example of faith is jumping off a high dive. My husband, CJ, tells a story of his first experience with the high dive when he was only eight or nine years old. In that phase of his life he loved going to the public swimming pool in his small town in the summer with his friends. As is common with most public pools, his pool had both a low dive and a high dive. One day, giving in to peer pressure, he decided to jump off of the high dive for the first time. Even today, he admits that he has a healthy fear of heights. However, on that particular summer day, his fear of heights got the best of him. As he climbed the ladder of the notorious high dive and saw how far he had to jump, fear took over. He stood on the high dive and contemplated whether or not he wanted to take the risk and jump. Ultimately, taking that step of faith would mean giving up his control and overcoming his fear. However, even with all his friends watching, he chickened out and slowly climbed back down the ladder of the high dive to the jeering of his friends.

1

Haven't we all experienced something like this in our lives as well? A moment where we have to decide if we are willing to step out in faith.

The good news about this story is that it does not end there. Later that day, CJ mustered up the courage to try the high dive once again. And this time, despite his fear, he jumped. And you know what happened? He loved it! Not only did he land safely in the water without injury, he also experienced the thrill of his lifetime. He then proceeded to jump off the high dive repeatedly for the rest of the day. In fact, he says eventually he became so daring that he would do all kinds of tricks off the high dive, including a one and a half twist dive.

What a great illustration of faith! Jumping off a high dive is simply one picture of stepping out in faith and the joy that comes as a result.

In this book you will read 21 different stories of faith from various authors. Sometimes the stories may focus on coming to faith in Christ for the first time. Other stories share lessons learned about faith during a difficult time.

Ultimately, we hope and pray that God uses these stories to inspire and encourage you in your own walk of faith. That by reading this book, your eyes will be fixed on Jesus, the author and perfecter of your faith, (Hebrews 12:2) allowing Him to strengthen your faith. Because "without faith it is impossible to please Him, for he who comes to God must believe that He is, and that He is a rewarder of those who diligently seek Him." ~Hebrews 11:6 (NKJV)

#1 An Unexpected Gift

By CJ Hitz

"And God will generously provide all you need. Then you will always have everything you need and plenty left over to share with others." - 2 Corinthians 9:8 (NLT)

Upon getting married in August of 1998, my wife Shelley and I were staring at a total of $58,000 in school loans between both of us. Fortunately, Shelley had secured a position as a Physical Therapist which would ease our financial burden while I finished my student teaching.

My teaching certification would be Secondary Ed. Social Studies which would allow me to teach History, Geography, Sociology, Psychology and Government. These are subjects I enjoyed growing up and I knew I could also enjoy teaching them to middle and high schoolers. But over the next few months, I began noticing a change in my desires. My zeal for planning and preparing 7th grade History lessons was slowly diminishing while my heart's passion was to study the Bible.

I found myself looking forward to finishing a History lesson so I could get back to devouring God's Word. My supervising teacher noticed this and sat me down to have a talk. I admitted to him that I hadn't devoted my best energy in preparing those lessons but I wasn't sure how I should handle this inner struggle. We both agreed that regardless of which direction I would go, I needed to stay focused and finish strong in my student teaching. Looking back, I'm thankful for the patience this outstanding teacher showed me.

After completing my teaching degree in November, I began doing some substitute teaching to bring in some extra income while seeking the Lord's direction for my life. As I was driving through town one day, I noticed a building with a sign that read, "Youth For Christ." I had first heard about this parachurch organization while taking a youth ministry class while at Anderson University. Still, I wasn't really familiar with what it was they did. After some deliberation, I decided to stop in and find out. "Certainly can't hurt," I thought to myself.

Paul, the Executive Director, greeted me at the door with enthusiasm. He invited me into his office where he proceeded to answer any questions I had while also introducing me to some of the staff. Their main mission and goal was to help lead students into a life-changing relationship with Christ. They did this by targeting un-churched students and inviting them to weekly meetings usually held in homes or some other neutral building. Each person on staff worked with one or two schools in the area where they also developed relationships with teachers, administrators and parents.

By the end of my time there, I was walking out the door with an application in my hand. Not only could I use the skills I learned in getting my education degree, I could also spend my time studying the Bible and preparing lessons geared toward drawing students closer to Jesus! The Lord was answering my heart's desire.

One detail that was mentioned up front was that each staff member was responsible for raising support, similar to a missionary. I was both excited and nervous about this prospect. After completing the application process, I was hired to work with two county schools. My salary would be a whopping $17,500 my first year which wasn't too much less than a first year teacher would make. Before I could actually begin, I had to have at least 50% raised in donations or monthly pledges. Between our church and several generous families, I was able to begin by March of 1999.

Youth For Christ had a policy where at the end of a staff person's first year, any amount received above their salary would be split 50/50. Half would go into the YFC general fund and half would be given to the staff person in the form of a check. "Cool!" I thought, not really thinking I would see anything extra.

Over the course of that first year, I found myself immersed in building relationships, planning weekly meetings, learning organization skills and just hanging out with teenagers. Most of my training was on the fly. Due to trainings and trips with students, Shelley and I were apart for a total of nearly two months in our first year of marriage. It's not something I recommend but the Lord was faithful to help us weather through that time.

As I mentioned in the beginning, we began our marriage with a hefty amount of school loans. Our goal was to pay our debt as quickly as possible. To do this, we had to live very simply. Our first apartment was a one bedroom, one bath unit within a tri-plex house. Our monthly rent ranged from $375-425 in the four years we lived there which was cheap, even for that time.

We also made a decision to try living on my meager $17,500 salary which translates to around $1,450/month. From the day we were married, we also dedicated ourselves to tithing on all our income. Time and time again, we experienced the Lord's blessing as we were faithful to give. Without a doubt, we saw the life of our cars and appliances extended. One of our cars had no business lasting as long as it did considering the wear and tear we put it through.

When the time came to file taxes for the first time as a married couple, we were excited to learn that we'd be receiving a refund of nearly $2,000. This was due to the fact that I was a student for most of 1998 and Shelley only had 6 months of Physical Therapy income. Unfortunately, we didn't have this refund the second time we filed taxes. Imagine our shock when we realized we were going to owe nearly $2,500 this time around! Ouch!

We had no savings since we were throwing every last penny into paying off those school loans. How would we pay? It was only weeks before this bomb was dropped in our laps that we sensed the Lord asking us to increase the amount we were giving. Did we hear you correctly Lord? Perhaps you meant for us to decrease our giving for a couple months? "Trust me, I know what I'm doing", said the Lord.

A couple weeks later I was sitting in my office when our Director, Paul, knocked on my door. "If you have a few minutes, I'd like to see you in my office", he said. "Did I do something wrong?" I thought to myself. Upon entering his office, I also noticed our Ministry Coordinator, Jim, sitting down. This definitely made me wonder what I did wrong. "Have a seat", they said. "Do you have any idea what this is about?" Jim asked. "Uhh…no," I responded. "It's time for your one year evaluation." This set my mind at ease as I realized I had nothing to worry about.

The three of us talked for about twenty minutes before Paul brought up the financial side of things. "You might recall our policy of writing a check for half the amount that you receive into your account above and beyond your salary?" To be honest, I had completely forgotten about this detail. He handed me an envelope and they both shook my hand. "Congratulations on making it through your first year," they said. "We're happy to have you on the YFC team."

Upon returning to my office, I slowly opened the envelope to see what it contained. Would it be $50? $100? I had no guess. As I pulled out the check and saw the amount, I was speechless. Three-thousand dollars! Are you kidding me? My eyes filled with tears as I recalled the Lord's words.

"Trust me, I know what I'm doing"

Not only did the Lord provide the amount we owed Uncle Sam in taxes, but He threw in an extra $500 for good measure. What an incredible lesson we learned that day early in our marriage. Our Heavenly Father longs to bless his children in ways we can't comprehend. Even when we can't see through our circumstances, we can trust the Lord to meet our needs.

Let's just say our faith was increased that day!

Bio:

CJ is an author, speaker and entrepreneur. In his downtime, he enjoys spending time outdoors running, hiking and exploring God's beautiful creation. You can find his books at www.BodyAndSoulPublishing.com

#2: Faith of a Child

By Mikayla Kayne

When the recession kicked off, it hit our blue collar town hard. Our business was failing, and we were in the process of losing our home and car. We had been struggling for over two years, sometimes living on thirty dollars a week and the kindness of others. We were learning what "living on faith" really means, and God was providing for us very much like he provided for the Israelites in the desert - just the basics, just enough, and just in time.

When our oldest son was eight, he had been dealing with our family's financial drought with amazing patience for a few years, but one Saturday morning he was especially discouraged. There was no food in the house, and he knew we had no money. As he sat quietly with his morning cartoons, letting us sleep, he prayed a simple prayer that somehow God would let him have breakfast.

As he told us later, it was only a few minutes before there was a knock at the door. Now, normally, he would have awoken us to answer it, but he peeked out and saw that it was one of our former business clients carrying a big box. My son opened the door and the man sat the box down and left without asking to see us. Inside that box was a gallon of milk, cans of spaghetti-o's, peanut butter and jelly, macaroni and cheese boxes, hot dogs and buns, juice, a loaf of bread, and a big box of Kids Crunch cereal. It was a box of kid food!

Our sweet boy was so hungry that he dug right in to the cereal and milk without a word. He put some of the groceries away and spent the rest of his morning basking in his answered prayer, and God's love that surrounded him in that moment. When my husband and I got up, we found him sitting on the coffee table with his arm resting in the box and eyes glazed over, not really watching the infomercial that had replaced his shows. When we took it all in, we were overwhelmed not only at our friend's generosity, but at how specifically every item in that box was hand-picked to minister to our son. We knew then that our hardship was serving a greater purpose, to teach him to trust God in a deep and personal way that most American kids never have to do.

That immediate answer to an honest prayer of need cemented my son's faith, and to this day he remembers how tangibly God can show up when we need Him. It's important to teach our kids to pray, and that they know God cares about every detail of their lives. He is always paying attention, and sometimes He answers their prayers in amazing ways so that they have their very own testimony of God's faithfulness to hold onto for a lifetime.

"Therefore I say to you, do not worry about your life, what you will eat or what you will drink; nor about your body, what you will put on. Is not life more than food and the body more than clothing? Look at the birds of the air, for they neither sow nor reap nor gather into barns; yet your heavenly Father feeds them. Are you not of more value than they?" - Matthew 6:25-26 (NKJV)

Bio:

Mikayla currently lives in Rochester, NY with her co-writer husband, Gregory Kayne, and their three sons. They are active in ministry, both speaking and leading worship for camps and special events. You can find them at: www.kaynecreative.com.

#3: A Journey to Doubtless Faith

By Mary L. Ball

Faith, such a simple word, but those five letters together conjure all sorts of meanings. As humans we have faith in lots of things. When we start our vehicle, we are confident that it will purr to life. Each day we flick a switch on the wall and believe that the lights will shine a glow brightening the room.

That's worldly assurance, something we all have. Putting your trust in God is the test of a true faith.

I remember back when I was seeking to become a published writer. I inscribe various flash stories and still produce weekly Christian articles; nevertheless, writing a fiction novel stretched my creativity.

Carving out an inspirational novel was a heart's desire. I wanted to use my writing, not only to reaffirm God's word, but to generate fictional characters that have everyday problems and overcome situations by the grace and mercy of Jesus Christ.

From the beginning to end, the process included four re-writes and lots of critiques. As with any debut author, doubts entered into my mind. I stood resilient in the Lord, replacing those uncertainties with faith.

For the next year, I held on to several verses from my King James Bible. The process of fine-tuning my manuscript crept on and rejection emails poured in from publishers.

As I would hit the delete button on my laptop and toss the notes in the trash, I voiced faith that a contract was on its way. I quoted one of my favorite stanzas from the book of Mark, placing emphasis on the words, "shall not doubt." The scripture is in chapter eleven, verse twenty-three.

"For verily I say unto you, That whosoever shall say unto this mountain, Be thou removed, and be thou cast into the sea; and shall not doubt in his heart, but shall believe that those things which he saith shall come to pass; he shall have whatsoever he saith." (KJV)

Furthermore, I believe there's power in the words we speak. In church, I declared to the congregation, testifying that I would become a published author.

"Death and life are in the power of the tongue: and they that love it shall eat the fruit thereof." - Proverbs 18:21 (KJV)

To me, speaking out a confirmation of the promises God offers is also a show of faith. The one important thing about having faith isn't standing in the belief of God's word for a while; it's having confidence in the assurances of the Lord's promises for the long haul. Faith must withstand time. It can't be a here today and gone tomorrow kind of trust.

The road to becoming a published author was long. It took a year and a half. Lots of re-writes and submitting to about fifty publishers.

Finally, the day came that I was offered a contract from a publisher willing to take a chance with a new author. I remember it was just before Christmas, and I fondly told my friends that even though it was Jesus' birthday I had received a Christmas present from Him.

I think back to those days and realize that when I faced my "mountain" of not being published, I took one day at a time and believed what is to come. Thank goodness, I had the strength not to waver.

In all our lives, we need to have a permanent belief that God can cause a change. Steadfast confidence is the key component to faith coming alive. What would have happened if I gave in to insecurities? For me, losing faith wasn't an option. I had a goal even though the world had objections. I know God has the final say, not men.

God wants good things for his children. If we abide in him, then he'll be true to us, so long as we aren't holding on to something that can be harmful to our growth as a follower of Christ. Maybe we don't get the results we want every time, but God's still in control. The Lord knows what's best for all of us.

We must hold on to our faith regardless of the mountain we perceive. Be certain, without a doubt; never give in to what the world says about you or the accomplishments you desire. Turn on the switch of faith by reading God's word and believe you can receive.

Bio:

Mary L. Ball is a published author of Inspirational Romantic Suspense and Mystery. Her novels inspire the enchantment of love, hope and a divine guidance that often lies dormant, waiting to be found by each of us. She often tackles subjects not common in Christian fiction. Nevertheless the subjects are shared by everyone in life. Writing Christian Articles keeps her focused on the real meaning of life. Contact her and find more about her books at http://MaryLouwrites.weebly.com.

#4: The Testament of Faith

By Nishoni Harvey

"The beginning of anxiety is the end of faith, and the beginning of true faith is the end of anxiety." --George Mueller

My dad was out of work due to an extensive knee surgery and ended up losing his job due to the recovery time. Times were tough, and money was hard to come by. They prayed fervently for God to provide another job for my father. Days turned into months and God had not yet seen fit to answer their prayers. They held to their faith in God and trusted in His promise that He would supply all their needs according to His riches in Glory by Christ Jesus. Still, my parents watched helplessly as the money in the bank and the food in the pantry dwindled. Soon, there was no food left in the house.

With two small children to feed, they set off for the river one day in hopes of catching enough fish for dinner. After many fruitless hours and with heavy hearts and dashed hopes, they started the short trek back home. They knew God wouldn't let them down. He had promised that He would provide, but all they had caught were two small brim. They carried them home, praying that it would be enough to satisfy my sister and me.

Upon returning home, they couldn't believe their eyes! The whole porch was covered with bags and bags of groceries! They wondered where the food had come from and how anyone knew they were in need. They had not told anyone, including family, about their financial situation. They had told no one, that is, except for God.

Attached to one of the bags was a tag that simply read, "From the three of us". My parents called everyone they could think of. No one would admit to leaving any packages on our stoop. Because God had rewarded their faith and provided where no one else could, we simply hold to the knowledge that it was a blessing and gift from God. We hold to our belief that "the three of us" who signed the tag on the bag was God the Father, God the Son, and God the Holy Spirit. What else can we think?

To this day, twenty-seven years later, we have never learned who our angels were, but we did learn a few new things. God always provides for His children. When the day seems dark and there seems to be no way out, look up. Have faith. Not only does God always have the answer, but God always is the answer.

In the years since, I've faced many trying times. My faith has been tested and stretched many times over, but God always reminds me of this story. The faith my earthly father held in my Heavenly Father still gives me reason to trust to this day. The way God rewarded that faith has always been a testament to me of how faith in God's promises will always pull me through, making me stronger in the end.

"I have been young, and now am old; yet have I not seen the righteous forsaken, nor his seed begging bread." --Psalm 37:25 (KJV)

Bio:

Nishoni Harvey is a saved, sanctified, and soul winning Baptist. She, her husband, Matthew, and their 3 young children serve faithfully at Hope Baptist Church of Harrison, Michigan, where they're active members. A graduate of Landmark Baptist College, Nishoni loves teaching, writing, playing with her instruments, and being a mommy. Nishoni is the author of THE FANATICS, which can be found at: www.amazon.com/gp/aw/d/B009XV1KEC

#5: A Broken Finger

By Ruth Kyser

I never thought I'd be thankful for a broken finger.

A number of years ago I was having an extremely difficult time in my job. I was going through a period of deep discouragement and depression, stuck in a career I'd fallen into which wasn't necessarily of my choosing. I eventually made the decision to mail out resumes and apply for some other jobs in the hopes that something better would come along. I could hardly wait!

Months went by and nothing seemed to happen and that just made me more upset with my job. Looking back on it now, I realize I was making myself absolutely miserable. A part of me must have realized this because I made the commitment to spend more time in prayer and Bible reading, hoping beyond hope to discover God's will. Did He want me to leave my current job and start a new career, or did He want me to stay where I was? And if He wanted me to stay, why was I so miserable?

I admit it, I'm human. When I didn't get a firm answer from God, I took it upon myself to make the decision without waiting for Him. I know – bad move! I decided if a job opportunity came along that was realistic, I was taking it. Shortly after that, I applied for a job at a school and believed after the first interview went well that it was supposed to be mine.

18

Then God spoke. Oh, I didn't hear His voice, but nonetheless, He spoke.

A misstep and the resulting tumble where my face met a concrete sidewalk resulted in a broken finger. There was little chance of me getting this new job now. Who was going to hire me with a splint on my finger? I couldn't type or write with that hand.

I wasn't very happy with God right then. Not only was I stuck in the job I was trying to get away from, but I was also going to have to do the job one-handed, and my broken finger hurt! It was a humbling experience for someone as independent as I am. Everything took me longer to accomplish. However, as I was forced to slow down, I began to look at it all differently – particularly my job. It was a good-paying job and instead of finding fault with it, I decided to be thankful for it – and for my bosses who appreciated my work (even my one-handed work). Suddenly, my attitude changed and consequently, so did my outlook on life.

I'd been looking for a sign from God all this time about what to do with my job. This is what I discovered: He didn't want me to change my job. He wanted me to change my attitude. When I finally did that, my whole outlook changed.

My faith in my Heavenly Father was restored. As always, He knew what was best for me even though I hadn't wanted to listen to Him. A broken finger had shown me He had me right where I was supposed to be. In hindsight I can tell you without a doubt that not leaving my job was for the best. Because of budget cuts, the position I was vying for at the school turned out to be temporary. If I had accepted that job, I would have soon been out of work.

During this time one of my favorite verses became Romans 8:28. I'd read it a hundred times, but as we so often do, I had never applied the words of the verse to my own life.

"And we know that all things work together for good to them that love God, to them who are the called according to his purpose." (KJV)

Do I believe God caused me to fall and break my finger? I don't believe He did, although He did take a bad event in my life and turned it into something for my good.

And for that broken finger, I will be forever thankful.

Bio:

Ruth Kyser is the author of several Christian fiction novels: "True Cover", "Endless Season", and "The Dove & The Raven". She enjoys telling stories that share how much God loves us.

You can connect with her on-line at her blog:
http://ruthkyser.wordpress.com

Or Facebook at:
http://www.facebook.com/authorruth.kyser

#6: Stepping Out of My Comfort Zone by Faith

By Krystal Kuehn

"I could never do that," I thought, as I listened to the music during the Sunday morning service. I thought it was courageous of Pat to volunteer to play the piano when the church had no one else. She hadn't played for very long, and she struggled through most of the songs. Then I couldn't help but think of how I had played the guitar and sang for many years; and yet, I was reluctant to volunteer. "When I feel ready," is what I would always say to myself. And now here was someone who did not wait to be "ready" or "good enough." She decided to serve God with her limited abilities. That is not just courageous; it is humbling. It takes humility and faith to be willing to fail and be less than perfect. It made me wonder if I was more concerned with what people thought than I was with giving God what I had.

The Lord was dealing with my heart concerning my attitude. James 4:10 (KJV) struck a chord in me: "Humble yourselves in the sight of the Lord, and he shall lift you up." Immediately my reaction was one of fear. I always associated humility with humiliation and embarrassment. "Oh please," I prayed, "Don't ask me so do something I can't do." Of course I knew that the Lord would never require that of his children. What I was actually praying was that I wouldn't be expected to do something that I didn't want to do or do something that was outside my comfort zone – something that would require me to humble myself before God and trust that He has my best interest at heart.

Over the years, I often confessed that I can do all things through Christ who gives me strength (Philippians 4:13). I didn't realize that now I needed strength to be humble. I never thought of myself as prideful. I was never out to show off or prove myself to anyone. But, as God spoke to my heart, I realized for the first time that God wanted me to be willing to sacrifice my pride to be obedient to Him. I soon had the opportunity to do just that in a way I least expected.

I prayed all week for an upcoming jazz session I was joining for the first time. I believed that God opened the door for this opportunity; so naturally, I wanted to be obedient. It was new to me and I knew it would be challenging, but I was confident that anything God had for me to do was possible with His help. It wasn't too difficult to trust and believe God as long as I felt comfortable and somewhat in control.

The jazz session turned out worse than I could have ever imagined. I didn't make it through a single song successfully. I felt like I failed miserably. I cried all the way home. "I can't do it," I told myself. It wasn't that I couldn't try real hard; learn from my mistakes, and eventually get it right. Rather, it was that I couldn't imagine being in a situation where I felt so humbled, and where my struggle and weaknesses were apparent to everyone.

As difficult as it would be, I knew I had to call my mentor who recommended me for the position. I told him that I was going to wait until I was "ready" and "good enough;" and I would try again then. He refused to let me quit. He refused to lose confidence in me. To my surprise, I couldn't talk my way out of it. He refuted my every argument until I felt completely drained and out of excuses. Hesitantly, I agreed to stay in the band.

Every time I thought about facing the band again, I felt a dreadful, sick feeling inside. It would have been so much easier to stay "comfortable." But deep inside I knew that if I was to trust God and walk by faith, I would have to grow and change; and there is no way of getting around the discomfort. I would have to walk by faith if I was going to be obedient. I would have to believe God in a way I never had before.

Then as I pondered the beauty of God's nature, I realized that He wants my ultimate best. He believes in me, and He doesn't give up on me no matter where I am at in my life. He doesn't want me to quit when I get uncomfortable. There is something He wants to do in me – something greater than I can imagine or comprehend. All I must do is submit to His will, and by faith, look past the present discomfort and pain. And God will take my circumstances and use them for His glory. The experience with the jazz band turned out to be one of the most rewarding and successful musical experiences I ever had. I not only grew in my faith, I grew as a musician. It prepared me for upcoming orchestral projects and much more. God's way is always the best if we would only believe!

I wondered about all the opportunities where I may have missed God by my lack of faith, times He wanted me to simply believe and trust Him to work out His plan for my life. It is so much easier to excuse ourselves, justify our complacency, or postpone what God would have us to do now to a time when we feel "ready." Unfortunately, that time seldom comes. The time to believe and serve the Lord is NOW. If we start with what we have, it is "good enough" for God.

Bio:

Krystal Kuehn, MA, LPC, LLP, NCC is a psychotherapist, best-selling author, teacher, musician and songwriter. Krystal specializes in helping people live their best life now, reach their full potential, overcome barriers, heal from their past, & develop a happiness lifestyle. Her inspirational and empowering approach has been helping people all over the world for over 20 years. Her books, articles, poetry, and songs have been published locally and internationally. Krystal has a passion for encouraging others. She believes everyone has untapped potential for greatness, and everyone can live a life of fulfillment and true happiness. Krystal is the co-founder of New Day Counseling in Michigan.

Her web sites include:
www.BeHappy4Life.com,
www.NewDayCounseling.org,
www.NewSongProductions.com,
www.Baby-Poems.com
as well as www.Facebook.com/WordsOfInspiration,
and Be Your Best blog
http://www.newdaycounselingcenter.blogspot.com.

#7: My Story of Faith

By Cliff Ball

God gave me the ability to write at a very young age, which sparked an interest in me when I was about eight after my parents bought me some novels to read. These included Robinson Crusoe, Treasure Island, Gulliver's Travels, a couple Christian-based young adult novels, and even the Little House series (my parents weren't readers, so they didn't think about the Little House series being mostly read by girls). The Little House TV series sparked an even bigger interest in me because it had just ended. I mostly became interested in Laura's story of how she became an author and I thought I wanted to do that too. So, after spending lots of time writing (in the age before e-mail) to the various places around the country where Laura used to live to find out how she came up with what she came up with, I began to write when I was ten. I wrote short stories here and there, submitted to various contests and magazines sporadically throughout the years, but never thought about doing anything serious with it. By the way, in my teens, I moved on from that interest in how Laura wrote, to being interested in reading and writing mostly science fiction novels (in case you're wondering).

Years later, as an adult in my 30's, my faith was tested when I was laid off from my job in October 2009. I had been praying and praying and applying for a job in a library for years, and then God finally granted me what I asked for. Unfortunately, I had moved to a new town specifically because I wanted to go to a particular church where the city happened to have a college to go to, but I slowly fell out of church once I got the job. I didn't realize this was a mistake until I'd been laid off, but I had faith that after I finished my last semester of college, which was the same year, that God would just up and grant me a new job.

That's not what happened. As a teenager, my parents had me pick a life verse, which I chose from Proverbs 3-5:6 KJV: "Trust in the Lord with all thine heart; and lean not unto thine own understanding. In all thy ways acknowledge him, and he shall direct thy paths." As an adult, I had a very hard time following this verse, because I really hadn't done any of that. I wanted to go my own way and I hardly ever gave God the acknowledgement in anything I did, whether I succeeded or failed. It would be a while before I realized that I had to rely completely on God.

At this same time, I had already published two novels thanks to the ease of the internet and being able to do it yourself, but I considered writing to be a hobby, nothing more. After being laid off, I felt God's influence and He was telling me to write Christian-based novels, but I didn't want to, and I ignored Him, because I wanted to write what I wanted to write. Because of that attitude, I wasn't very successful as a published author. I also hadn't had very much success finding a new job, so I was incredibly discouraged, but figured that I needed to return to college to get my GPA up so that I could get a Master's in Technical Communication, and then someone would hire me. All that did was get me deeper in student loan debt, since I didn't get accepted into the MTC program at the University I was going to here in Texas. Instead of doing what God wanted me to do or even praying about it, which was write Christian-based novels, I got into deeper trouble.

In late 2011, I finally started listening to what God wanted, but it took my mom, who wasn't a writer, or a reader for that matter, but a very strong Christian, to help steer me to what God wanted me to do. God gave her an idea for a story which I kept dismissing, so she ignored me (for which I'm grateful), and wrote down an outline for the entire thing. She gave it to me around Thanksgiving, but I was still really hesitant to write the novel. My attitude was: Who reads anything Christian besides the Left Behind series? But, after Christmas, I decided I would give it a shot. Boy was I surprised when I started writing. The story flowed out of me, to the point where I didn't want to stop writing, and I could feel God's influence as I was writing it. This felt odd to me, mostly because I hadn't really felt His presence like that since I was a child. I usually write every few days or once a week before this, but I wrote every day, sometimes more than five hours at a time, on this novel for thirty days straight.

When I was done, I felt drained of energy, but I finally felt like I did something that God had wanted me to do for a long time. Then, I published the novel, Times of Trouble, a few weeks later. I was astounded that it took off, since the doubting Thomas in me thought it would never sell, and ever since, the novel has been selling on average two a day between Amazon and Barnes & Noble. I don't know why exactly, but writing that novel helped me to see that I should have faith in God's plans for me, even though I don't know where He's taking me on this journey as a writer. I look forward to it.

Bio:

Cliff Ball is a born again Christian and is a member of his local Baptist church. Cliff first became published in high school in the early 90's, and has published nine novels and two short stories. Please visit his website at www.cliffball.net.

#8: Can We Have Faith After Tragedy?

By Ada Brownell

The baby was having trouble in the hospital delivery room. Every time my daughter pushed, the infant's oxygen shut off. The cord was too short and trapped between the child's head and the birth canal.

Our son–in-law stuck his head out the door. "Now would be a good time to pray."

His parents and we began to pray. My faith, I admit, was shaky as my mind imagined my daughter's grief if the baby were stillborn. Since we lost a child to an aggressive form of cancer, when I approach God's throne I'm aware He allows us to go through difficulty sometimes. Could I have faith after tragedy? I knew I believed God is the "rewarder of those who diligently seek Him" and "the worlds were framed by the word of God, so that the things that are seen were not made out of things which are visible." Both of those phrases come from Hebrews 11—the Bible's faith chapter.

So aware God was listening, I bound fear and loosed my faith. In moments, a cry came from the next room. The baby was fine.

Since then, I've increased Bible study. We've seen more miracles. Less than two years after that baby was born, during another pregnancy our daughter developed gall bladder trouble. The physician warned she might need surgery while pregnant. We prayed and she was able to wait until after the birth. Then our daughter was thought to have multiple sclerosis. Later tests showed she's fine. We've had many other miracles in our large family (one of them comfort after our oldest daughter's death), but I need to continue to build my faith.

Max Lucado paraphrases Hebrews 11 (NIV) in his article, "What Faith Sees": He says, "Faith is trusting what the eye can't see. Eyes see the prowling lion. Faith sees Daniel's angel. Eyes see storms. Faith sees Noah's rainbow. Your eyes see your faults. Your faith sees your Savior. Your eyes see your guilt. Your faith sees His blood." (http://www.thoughts-about-god.com)

I decided to research faith. This is what I found:

1. Our Creator wrapped faith in our DNA. Dr. Andrew Newberg, neuroscientist and author of "Why We Believe What We Believe," says our brains seem to have a special place for faith. He has tracked how the human brain processes religion and spirituality. It's all part of a new field called neurotheology. Newberg says the frontal lobe, the area right behind our foreheads, helps us focus our attention in prayer and meditation. The parietal lobe, located near the backs of our skulls, is the seat of our sensory information. He says this place in the brain is involved in that feeling of becoming part of something greater than oneself. The limbic system, nestled deep in the center, regulates our emotions and is responsible for feelings of awe and joy.

Newberg says similar areas of the brain are affected during prayer and meditation. He suggests brain scans may provide proof that our brains are built to believe in God. He says there may be universal features of the human mind that actually make it easier for us to believe in a higher power.

I believe people search for God because of the "God-shaped void" within. If they haven't heard the gospel or reject it, they worship the earth, an idol they know is nothing but a figure humans created, or devise their own religion—even making unbelief into doctrine.

2. God has given each person the ability to believe and his own lump of faith. "For I say, through the grace given to me, to everyone who is among you, not to think of himself more highly than he ought to think, but to think soberly, as God has dealt to each one a measure of faith." (Romans 12:3 NKJV).

3. Faith arises from the need to know our Heavenly Father. Since the Lord gave humankind a choice of whether to serve Him, God prevents us from "proving" He exists and leaves that and other vacancies for our faith to fill.

4. Faith comes through hearing the Word—the gospel. The Apostle Paul wrote "Faith comes by hearing the message, and the message is heard through the word of Christ" (Romans 10:17 NIV). "All scripture is given by inspiration of God, and is profitable for doctrine, for reproof, for correction, for instruction in righteousness" (2 Timothy 3:16 KJV).

5. Faith results from acting on what was heard. Romans 10:9 (NIV) says, "If you declare with your mouth, 'Jesus is Lord,' and believe in your heart that God raised him from the dead, you will be saved."

6. Faith comes through the will. We decide whether to believe God's Word, a false religion, or atheism. Everything about

who we are, why we are here and where we are going takes faith. Yet it takes a leap—a decision.

7. Faith is created by combining belief with common-sense actions. James calls it "faith and works" (James 2:22).

8. Faith develops out of our hopes. We hope for something, but it takes faith to receive it.

9. Faith can come as a fruit and Gift of the Holy Spirit. (Galatians 5:22, 1 Corinthians 12:9).

10. Faith comes from a combination of our will to believe and the Holy Spirit's revelation. The Word must be planted, watered, and then our lives bear fruit.

Bio:

Ada Brownell has written for Christian publications since age 15 and spent much of her life as a newspaper reporter. She is the author of the teen novel Joe the Dreamer: The Castle and the Catapult - http://buff.ly/XeqTvH; and Swallowed by LIFE: Mysteries of Death, Resurrection and the Eternal - http://amzn.to/Jnc1rW.

#9: Faith that Can Move Mountains

By Amanda Penland

November and December of 2011 was exhausting. Trips to the ER and doctor were not uncommon. A week before Christmas my husband Tony was in the ER for the 3rd time due to severe dehydration from his new blood pressure medication. While the doctor asked him questions he told him about a lump he had recently discovered. A urologist was called in to run tests. The urologist was supposed to let him know the results as soon as possible. The next day he was sent home to rest.

He hadn't been his normal active self for a while due to the dehydration. I couldn't wait any longer. The suspense was killing me. So, on Christmas Eve I asked him, "Have you heard from the doctors yet?" I knew from the look he had on his face it wasn't good. He told me he got the letter a few days before. He just didn't want to tell me till after Christmas. He said he would need to have surgery to remove the mass. They weren't sure of the exact type or if it was spreading. I broke down.

On Christmas day, our pastor's wife gave out mustard seeds as the pastor spoke about having faith like a grain of mustard seed. I went right home and printed out the verse Matthew 17:20 (KJV): "And Jesus said unto them, because of your unbelief: for verily I say unto you, If ye have faith as a grain of mustard seed, ye shall say unto this mountain, remove hence to yonder place; and it shall remove; and nothing shall be impossible unto you."

I posted it with the mustard seed on our fridge. Every time we passed by it we would pray and even touch the seed. I got on my knees telling God I had faith that he would heal Tony. I knew He could confine his cancer and keep it from spreading to the rest of his body. I asked God to be with the doctors and help them to remove all the cancer from his body.

We went to talk with the urologist about the upcoming procedure and the type of testicular cancer it could be. I was so numb and I hurt so much I couldn't comprehend. When you hurt it's hard not to doubt. When we got home the tears fell. Tony and I held each other and prayed. A week before his surgery, praise God, his tumor moved! On January 10, 2012 the doctors removed it all. The urologist said it was confined only to that one area. Tony has so far been cancer free since his surgery.

Bio:

Amanda is a stay-at-home mom of five, house wife, and Blogger at http://LordLeadMeOn.blogspot.com.

#10: Three Ways to Exchange Fear for Faith

By Janet Perez Eckles

The other day while my fingers danced on my keyboard, suddenly something happened. My muscles tightened. "Cindi, I don't know what's wrong," I wrote to my friend and ministry partner. "I'm stuck, really stuck. My computer says there's no room on the disk and I'm out of memory."

Even from far away, she resolved the crisis. "Sometimes," she wrote gently, "this can happen when you have too many windows open."

Duh! That's exactly what happened. I, the queen of multi-tasking, had so many windows open at once that a mighty draft was probably blowing my way.

Why do we do that? It's insane. We open windows in life too—our kids do something off-the-wall for the umpteenth time, we open the window of worry. When will they ever learn! Money problems don't let up, so we open the window of anxiety. The doctor's office leaves a message, "We found something abnormal in the test." We open the window of fear. Our spouse still won't understand us; we fling open the window of anger.

Then our life gets stuck, no more memory of joy. The files where peace was stored can't be accessed. And the folder of security is empty.

Frustration led me to find a 3-step solution:

1.) Take a deep breath, look up. The God of the universe is watching. He's listening and ready to point to the solution.

2.) Pull emotionally away from all those open windows.

3.) Inhale His comfort, repeat His promise and know that, "Though I am surrounded by troubles, you will bring me safely through them" (Psalm 138:7, The LB-Paraphrased).

Father, in the midst of fear that fuels my stress, how comforting it is to know that You, with Your mighty power, will bring me safely through all those stages. Teach me to trust in You, in your timing and in Your ways, as You show me how to purposefully close the window of fear brought on by adversity. In Jesus's name, Amen.

Bio:

Best-selling author and international speaker, Janet Perez Eckles offers personal success coaching. Your free, 30-minute coaching session with her is just a click away: www.janetperezeckles.com.

#11: Like Pine, Like Pain

By Jorja Davis

Last week a crash of thunder in the night marked the moment when all our plans for the next day would make an abrupt shift. It was the moment when an eighty-foot pine tree went twisting and crashing and fell across our backyard. Rather than turning the soil in the garden for planting pumpkins with the grandchildren, my husband cleaned and oiled the chainsaw to remove the tree lying across the children's garden. That sudden shift of priority reminded me of a not-so-subtle shift, when after three months of aggressive treatment for pain, the word cure disappeared and the word management took its place. It was a shock, a thunderclap.

Eighteen years ago, I had minor surgery. Four weeks after the surgery, my life came crashing down around me. I developed a major complication that would soon become chronic and then intractable. Reflex Sympathetic Dystrophy created profound changes that overshadowed my life and living. Instead of sewing 5000 seed pearls on our older daughter's wedding dress and packing for our last military tour in Germany, almost every day I rode 80 miles round trip in excruciating, burning pain to the John Hopkins Medical Research Hospital's Pain Management Clinic.

Somehow among all the lumbar sympathetic blocks that had their own pain, I found myself leaning more and more into Jesus' arms. Every time, I had to sign a sheet of paper explaining the possible outcomes of the treatment. The last phrase was always "even death." I knew I won either way, but thank goodness I learned to put my head on Jesus' shoulder and let Him wrap His arms around me, especially on the day when all the students came to observe. In addition to the x-rays he used to help position the needle, the doctor used contrast dye so the students could better see the procedure. It turned out I was allergic to the dye. No better place to disappear into anaphylaxis than in a room with 8 doctors, being held by the Great Physician.

When we arrived in Germany, the blocks were administered by an anesthesiologist in the surgical recovery room in the Army Hospital, where all injured soldiers are triaged and treated before returning to their units or home countries. He did not use x-ray. Because he had worked twenty years in military hospitals, he had done thousands of lumbar sympathetic blocks on soldiers who had lost limbs, suffered crush traumas, or gunshot wounds. I found myself burying my head in Jesus' shoulder, grasping two-fists-full of his garments. Praying aloud through every treatment right up to the day the nurses were putting up Christmas decorations.

This was the day the interns rotated into the recovery room. The anesthesiologist laughed and joked as he began the procedure. This time the doctor nicked a blood vessel. The steroids and lidocaine rushed to my heart, my lungs, and my brain. The room began to spin, I could see fireworks on the ceiling, and I could not breathe. The anesthesiologist called for saline fluid and a nurse to start an IV in my arm. Quietly at first and then increasing in volume I heard Amy Grant singing Breath of Heaven. "Breath of heaven hold me together, be forever near me. Hold me together. Hold me." God's presence has never been more real or palpable.

Like taking a chainsaw to the tree, eighteen years of living with chronic pain has cut my self-identity down to holy size...to what God sees. My day planner has been converted from allotments of time to chunks of energy. My priorities have tumbled from many to one at a time. Before pain consumed my days and nights, I often forgot I am not defined by what I do, but by who and whose I am. Pain is, among other things, clarifying.

Everything that is planned or scheduled will take time and energy. And even if I know how much energy is needed, I will not know how much energy I will have to spend until I wake up. I know it will take two hours to stretch my muscles and get my stiff joints moving. If I use those two hours to stretch my body and direct my focus away from pain toward God, I stay more relaxed and more ready to deal with scheduled events and falling trees.

The pain remains. The deterioration of body continues. Some mornings my Bible is too heavy to hold. Some mornings my fingers will not turn a page. Some mornings I just light a candle scented with myrrh and sit and immerse myself in the smell of a gift of pain and memory--and in words of hope remembered:

"Be still and know that I am God." (Psalm 46:10 NIV)
"Come to me all you who are weary." (Matthew 11:28 NIV)

The principles haven't changed. They are just narrowed from plural to singular:

* balance goal and priority;
* set a manageable task according to available energy;
* leave some slack to deal with the unexpected – such as fallen trees.

The tree fell a week ago. A large part of it still lies across the backyard right up to the edge of the pumpkin patch. I can smell the pine when the back door is opened. The dark earth-bound roots are turning a rain-washed gray. Someday my husband will return to the task of sawing the rest into movable chunks. The tree will be cut and gone only when it becomes the priority, goal, and critical task of the day. Today we need to plant pumpkin seeds with the grandchildren.

Like pine, like pain, well-managed, I pray.

Bio:

Jorja Davis is a retired librarian and teacher. Her chronic pain leaves her plenty of time to read, write reviews, blog, and quilt. God seems always to send people to nurture. Today her greatest joy is daughters who encourage her to be deeply involved in the lives and faith of their children.
http://jorjaadavisthewriterreads.blogspot.com
http://jorjaadaviscommonprayer.blogspot.com
http://jorjaadavisnana911.blogspot.com

#12: No Limits

By Kim Bookmyer

"For nothing is impossible with God." Luke 1:37 (NLT)

The Lord has been patiently trying to teach me the TRUTH of this verse over the last several years. Recently He took me on a mission trip to Nicaragua to show me once again that with Him there are NO LIMITS!

With God - there are NO language barriers, age barriers, cultural barriers, physical barriers, economic barriers, relationship barriers, denominational barriers, _____(fill in the blank). When we put our trust in Him, He is well able to take down all of those barriers so that we may experience His unconditional, passionate love for all people!

I may have a language barrier as I don't speak Spanish BUT God doesn't! He was showing me that His love can be communicated in a smile, a touch, through a provision of food, an embrace, a prayer, worship. God brought to us Nicaraguans who love Jesus and traveled with us to be our interpreters. Often though there were not enough interpreters and we were dependent on the Holy Spirit to lead us and guide us as we prayed for people.

God understands all languages. As we prayed for people it was amazing to watch God break through walls that were in their lives and to bring healing and comfort to them. We were complete strangers; asking God to touch them at the root of their pain, doubt, fear, brokenness. And right in front of us, we could see the power of the Holy Spirit consuming them. A person's countenance would completely change and after prayer there would be an unspeakable joy; a transformed life! A new follower of Christ or a hurting brother or sister who left knowing that God was their provider, comforter, healer! We may not have known what happened but the Creator who "knit them together fearfully and wonderfully" (Psalm 139:13-14 paraphrased) sure touched them. There are NO LIMITS with God.

In the United States we've put up a barrier for God in our educational system. In Nicaragua, it is still permissible to come into the public schools and share the gospel message and pray with the students. So often we did our outreach in public schools. The students shared music, dramas and testimonies of how the Lord has changed their lives and then there would be an altar call for prayer. They were hungry for God and many would come for prayer!

At one of the schools, I noticed a couple teachers standing in a doorway. I felt led to go pray with them. After finding someone to ask them if they would like prayer, one teacher left. I was wondering what happened but in a moment I found out that she was getting the principal and soon the entire teaching staff was standing in the office wanting prayer. God had made a way for me, a former 5th grade teacher from Ohio, to pray for these beautiful teachers in Nicaragua! Only God knew that one day I would be in Nicaragua praying with other teachers! There are NO LIMITS with God in the school systems.

We may have put up barriers in our government and in the church but God was showing me His heart to be involved! Several years ago, God showed me that as believers we are called to uplift our pastors in prayer and to encourage them in the Lord for they have a difficult job shepherding us sheep and to also pray for our governmental leaders for His wisdom. We were in one community where the mayor, a man of God, had coordinated with the local pastors to seek God together. We were at the mayors' office for lunch and 12 pastors (from different denominations) had taken the day to spend with us. They traveled to the different schools and then we were all part of an evangelistic crusade for the entire community that evening where there must have been 900 people worshiping God together. God provided me an opportunity to pray with the pastors. One shared with me how the Lord has been bringing unity to their community by bringing the pastors together. They meet to pray with one another regularly including the mayor! Where there is unity, God will command the blessing! There are NO LIMITS with God in the government or the church.

One day, we were waiting to cross a river to get to one of the villages where we were sharing the good news of Jesus Christ and feeding the children. I was pondering how I was going to cross the river. The youth were jumping to the other side but I was sizing up the width and thinking...I'm getting wet! Then in the distance I could see this man, carrying a plank. He made a bridge for the remainder of us to cross. God provides a way. Seeing that man made me think of Jesus who provides the way...the way to a relationship with our Creator! He carried a cross, was crucified and lives again so that we may cross over....effortlessly because of His great sacrifice. He is the God that transcends all barriers and it is only because of His Son, Jesus Christ's death, resurrection and ascension that all things are possible with Him. It is because He did not leave us alone but gave us Himself in the person of the Holy Spirit to live within us now...so that we may have LIFE ABUNDANTLY now and forevermore!

Brothers and sisters in Christ, with God there are NO LIMITS! Seek Him with all that you are. Ask Him every morning to break your heart over the things that break His heart and to fill your heart with His love, to give you eyes to see as He sees and ears to hear His voice above all the other voices in the world. He has great plans for you....be amazed at where and how the Father desires to use you for His glory...for His Kingdom purposes. This mom from Ohio is amazed to see how the Lord has transformed me and took me to Nicaragua to share His love with others. For there is NOTHING that is impossible with God! (Luke 1:37) He is LIMITLESS! Believe that there are NO LIMITS with God!

Bio:

Kim Bookmyer is a wife, mother, daughter, sister, friend BUT most importantly a daughter of the King!

#13: Little Footsteps

By Mark Moyers

Ah the good ole' days; I remember them fondly. It was a time when my relationship with God was just beginning to bloom. Everything was new, exciting, and full of possibilities. God was filling me with His word and His Spirit as never before. Like a sweet summer day the glory of God washed over me, and everything was right with the world.

Thinking back on it, that was a pretty good weekend. Soon after, God enrolled me in spiritual boot camp. What's spiritual boot camp you say? Well, a good example is when God taught me the meaning of 2 Corinthians 5:7 (NIV)…

"For we live by faith, not by sight."

My lesson began with an ordinary evening out. A small group of people and I had gone out to eat one evening. A movie might have been involved as well, but to be honest, I really can't remember. You see, there was something else that captured my attention that night.

Over the course of the evening, somewhere between the breadsticks and the good-natured ribbing, the subject of abortion arose. It was a short exchange between a close friend and her boyfriend, only lasting for a moment. There were no heated exchanges or sharp disagreements, and yet, there was something about it that stood out to me. I was troubled by it, but I didn't understand why.

The evening passed quickly, but what I had experienced that night persisted long after the leftovers were gone. Try as I might, I couldn't shake the uneasiness I was feeling. Pushing it out of my thoughts was only temporary as it always had a way of creeping back in.

I tried to rationalize it, reason with whatever was happening. I knew my friend well; she was a Christian whose character matched her beliefs. She respected life and would never have an abortion. Yet, that wasn't enough to make it stop. On and on this went until it finally became clear what was happening.

In the night, in the middle of the darkness and the silence, that still small voice spoke deep into my spirit.

"Tell her."

Instantly I realize it had been God speaking to me all along, and now He wanted me to remind her of what she already knew. I didn't understand why, so I wrestled with God. I gave Him all the usual excuses – she's a Christian, she already knows, she might get angry with me – but He would have none of it. Just when I had almost completely pushed it out of my mind, He spoke again.

"Tell her!"

This time a little louder and more insistent. Again I offered my excuses and managed to push it down one more time – enough to make it comfortable for myself. Several times God spoke to me; each time was a bit louder and more insistent than the last. When He spoke my spirit would ring and my body would shudder making it impossible to miss His voice. This persisted until one final time.

"TELL HER!"

The prophet Jeremiah wrote that God's word was like a fire shut up in his bones (Jeremiah 20:9) and I wondered what it was like to feel what Jeremiah was describing. When this last command came, I finally knew. And just like Jeremiah, I too could no longer hold what God had given me, so I relented.

I told God He would have to guide me in what to say, and He did just that. But out of fear I couldn't speak to her directly. If you have ever tried to deliver God's message to someone, you would know why. So I wrote it in a letter and mailed it.

A couple weeks later I received a phone call; she had called to talk about what I wrote. She wasn't angry, but she was a bit confused, much like me. I assured her I already knew what she believed, but I felt the need to remind her. She accepted that, and after some small talk we parted once again.

As you might have guessed, our conversation didn't bring me any clarity. I still had no idea what the purpose of this was, or even if there was a purpose. And after we hung up I thought to myself, "I wonder why God had me do that." Immediately, God spoke once again.

"She is going to have a baby."

What?! God, how? She isn't married, she isn't even engaged! Plus she is saving herself for marriage! I had just received an answer from God about "why" – a rather rare answer to receive – and it only brought me more questions. So, I did what any other rational person would do in my position – I decided I must be crazy and did my best to forget about it. And it worked. That is, until the tables were turned.

Months later, it was my turn to receive something in the mail. It was... a wedding invitation. Yes, you guessed it – my friend and her boyfriend, the same one that was with us that night, were getting married. Once I regained consciousness the natural line of questioning ensued. Could it really be? Was God's word fulfilled? Is she... is she really?

For months I wondered, right up until the day of the wedding. As the time drew near I counted the moments.

Tick... I arrive at the church.
Tock... I'm standing in the foyer.
Tick... I make my way to a pew – an aisle seat.
Tock... The groom and groomsmen enter.
Tick... The music starts.
Tock... The sanctuary doors open...

She's thin! Hallelujah! Finally, closure! What a relief, I must have been wrong, and I'm glad. Now I can put this whole thing behind me, and I will never have to deal with anything like this ever again.

Six weeks after the wedding I had the chance to talk with my newly married friend on the phone. We spoke about how the wedding went, where they went on their honeymoon, and "oh by the way, did I mention I'm pregnant?" What!? Already? "Yep, that quickly." She continued, "...and my husband wants me to have an abortion."

Instantly, all of the pieces fall into place. Humbled, and in awe of God's amazing goodness, we hang up and I hear that still small voice one more time.

"See?"

Looking back, it was such a small step of faith that pales in comparison to some of the things God has had me do since. But of course, first steps always do. On that day, no mountains were moved, no seas were parted, but one blind man received his sight. The oh-so-small amount of discomfort I experienced paled in comparison to the priceless lesson I learned.

I don't know if what God directed me to do changed the course of events, but I don't have to know, for we walk by faith, not by sight. What I do know is, God knows what He is doing, and my friend's baby girl is doing just fine.

Bio:

Mark is a minister, a mentor, a leader and more. Called by God at an early age, Mark has walked a long and difficult road few have chosen to travel. If there is a hallmark of Mark's life and ministry, it is his desire to help people live free and receive all God has for them.

Read more stories about Mark's journey with God and the insights God has given him in his book, "Who Is This God Anyway?: One Man's Pursuit of God and the Wonders He Discovered (2013)" Find it and more at: WhoIsThisGodAnyway.com.

#14: Desires of the Heart

By Lilly Maytree

My husband and I fell in love with boats early in our marriage, and owned several over the years. They ranged from our first twenty-three-foot sailboat on a nearby lake, to an ocean-going sloop twice that size when our children were teenagers and made up a great crew. Having tried pretty much everything, we dreamed of having a traditional ketch with classic lines, small enough for just the two of us to handle, but could still go anywhere in the world.

Of course, that kind was incredibly expensive, and life distracted us with many things that were more important. However, when the freedom of retirement came along, we started dreaming, again. Then, one summer, we set out to discover if "divine appointments" were real (I had recently written a novel on that theme), and unknowingly embarked on the adventure of a lifetime.

It began as a book tour. But it was more than that, really, because we didn't exactly know where we were going, or what our final destination would be. And because it was as much a mystery to us as anyone else, we called it a "mystery tour." Did God have any real divine appointments lined up for us? And if so, how would we recognize them?

I've heard when traveling through new territory, it's best to follow someone who knows where they're going. So, we began looking for the "footsteps of God" ahead of us, in order to make sure we stayed to the right path. These were the little things that worked out with such perfect timing that we couldn't possibly have arranged ourselves. We had been rescued this way during many emergencies of our lives and called them miracles because there was simply no other way to explain them. Could the same thing work for dreams?

Next thing we knew, that long ago dream became very intense. But, living on a fixed income, we were in no position to buy a sailboat. Still, times being what they were, there might be someone out there who desperately needed to get rid of one. And one of the surest signs of "God's footsteps" was that His provisions usually met the needs of more than just us at the same time. So, we began to look from one end of the state to the other, at any and all boats that might fit the requirements.

First of all, there would have to be no money down, because we didn't have any. In fact, we had to rent our house out just to have enough in the budget for all the extra traveling it would take to find the thing. Then the owner would have to agree to carry financing on it, because we would never qualify for a bank loan. Not to mention we needed immediate possession since we had no place to live anymore. For heaven's sake, what were we thinking? And whose idea was it to blast it all over the internet by way of documentation so when this tremendous "miracle" happened, there would be no question it was God (and not us) who did it?

I could write an entire book on the potential this "mystery tour" had for being extremely embarrassing, but we won't go there. The important thing is that God did show up. The reason I know is because -- well, for heaven's sake -- I better not go there, either. Instead, I'll just jot down a "list of footsteps," and let you decide for yourself...

51

After weeks of looking, the only thing we found was where we would put a boat if we actually ever got one. It was a beautiful historical old waterfront on Liberty Bay.

We eventually ran out of gas money to look for more boats, so the Captain answered an ad in a Seattle newspaper for a part-time job to get some. It turned out to be next to Liberty Bay. It also turned out to have a couple hundred others who applied, but they chose my senior-age husband over all of them. What kind of job? Repair and replace roofing on commercial buildings. At an amazingly high wage.

During this "lull" in our hunt, I posted a picture of our original "dream boat" (on the blog) that I took from a sales catalog, simply because I had run out of real boats to look at. It was of a thirty-two foot Mariner ketch.

We stumbled onto a neglected version of that boat (right on Liberty Bay!) but it wasn't for sale. We tracked down the owner, anyway. Turns out he had health problems and couldn't keep it up. We made him an offer; he countered with A LOWER ONE, and AGREED TO ALL OUR TERMS.

There was a waiting list to get into the marina, but because the boat had been there for fourteen years, and the owner was friends with the harbor master, we got to stay in the same place for... half the current rate.

The Captain's job was less than a mile away from that location.

The former owner (also on a fixed income) was able to move into a better home with the extra money.

The boat cleaned up beautifully, and was completely paid off within a few months.

It was a thirty-two foot Mariner ketch... just like in the picture.

At this point you might wonder how all these amazingly "mysterious coincidences" affected our faith. Well, I'll tell you. The truth is, following in God's footsteps is extremely exciting. There's absolutely nothing else like it when it comes to adventure. So, we've decided we're not going home this year. Instead... we're going on.

"Delight yourself in the Lord: and he shall give you the desires of your heart. Commit your way to the Lord; trust also in him; and he shall bring it to pass."
Psalm 37:4-5 (NKJV)

Bio:

Lilly Maytree is an inspirational adventure novelist who is living out her dreams aboard the GLORY B. You can follow along with her by visiting
http://www.LillysArmchairTravelers.blogspot.com.

A list of her books is available at www.LillyMaytree.com.

#15: My Close Encounter of the God Kind

By Carol Freed

I knew I should have skipped this class! "Learning to Tell Your Faith Story in Three Minutes." What an embarrassing situation this was turning into for me!

Here I was in Washington DC in 1988 at a national evangelism training conference. I did not see myself as an "evangelist," so I came to provide adult supervision of sightseeing for teens from my home church in Oregon. Besides, what "faith story" did I have?

I have no memory of not knowing about Jesus Christ as God's son and my Savior and believing the Bible to be true. My faith in God has been the foundation for my entire life. About age 7, I read the story of Solomon asking God for wisdom. That really impressed me – so I asked God: "Please give me your wisdom – if it is OK to ask for that - even though I don't expect to be as wise as Solomon!"

But asking for wisdom like Solomon probably would not qualify as the kind of "faith story" this class leader wanted. Let me think - what would be worthwhile to tell someone?

All my relatives were Lutherans, so being a believer was just the way our family lived. I liked going to church, reading my Bible and having simple conversations with God. I sang in choir and attended a Christian elementary school.

54

Oops, I better listen...what was he saying? Break up into pairs and practice our faith story...yuck!

What should I do now? Too late to sneak out the door! Really, why would anyone want to hear about my journey of faith?

While everyone was finding a partner, I quickly rummaged through the file cabinet of my mind looking for clues on what to say. Suddenly a friendly woman in her 30's sat down by me. Inspiration came quickly...just have her tell her story first. Maybe she will use all our time and I won't have to say anything.

Before she started, I mentally challenged God. "I'll bet she has a dramatic life-and-death kind of story, which will prove I have no story worth telling to anyone. Definitely should have skipped this class!"

Her first words were indeed dramatic. "A few years ago, I decided to kill myself." She continued: "I heard a TV preacher say, 'God loves you and you are precious to Him. He can make your life worth living.' So I asked God, if He was real, to give me the strength to get through that night. I promised to ask Jesus into my life and learn what that means." She used all our time together.

Taking on a smug attitude, I challenged God again: "See, I was right!" Hoping the class would be over soon, I was shocked when the leader told us to find a new person to practice our faith stories. This time I listened to a young man about 19. He was so on fire for God that he radiated an electric kind of energy as he talked. He had been on drugs and in a gang before becoming a Christian.

"See, God, I don't have a meaningful story. I'll be so happy to get out of this class!" I allowed him to take up all our practice time, again managing to escape sharing my insignificant "faith story."

Then it happened - like the voice of God Himself talking directly to me! The leader said: "Perhaps a few of you here are like me, receiving the blessings of being raised in a Christian family, always attending church and loving God, and feeling you have no dramatic or worthwhile story to tell anyone." By now, both God and the leader had my total attention. I could feel my heart pounding. This would be a rare opportunity to get an immediate answer from God.

The leader continued: "So what kind of faith story do we have? Our testimony is simple: 'Faith works.' We can tell people that it is possible to be raised in a Christian home, learn to love God and not go through spiritual rebellion. We can encourage people by sharing how faith is foundational to all that we do and think. We should not be ashamed of being able to explain what God's power can do, especially when it is applied to everyday life. God often uses many people to talk with a person before they become a believer. You might be a great example of a life-long Christian that a person needs to meet. The Holy Spirit will bring to you exactly the right people to hear your unique story."

I felt inspired as I realized my faith story was worthwhile after all! The Holy Spirit opened my heart to understand what I had just heard. Imagine! God cared enough about me to bring me here to learn such an important lesson. Immediately I asked God for forgiveness of my cynical comments.

My response was a simple prayer: "Dear God, I believe You revealed a new truth to me - that being raised in a Christian home is a powerful and useful faith story. I'll trust the Holy Spirit to bring to me the people who need to hear what I have experienced."

Was my prayer answered? Absolutely! Many times since then, the Holy Spirit has led me to share my story, specifically with mothers, to encourage them to model their faith in their family life because - "It works!"

My conversations with mothers have varied from a hospital bed to PTA meetings, on vacation and at conferences, but mostly in grocery stores! Nothing compares to the thrill of experiencing another close encounter of the God kind in these prearranged meetings. I am so thankful that I didn't skip that training class!

Psalm 71:17 NLT - "Oh God, you have helped me from my earliest childhood, and I have constantly testified to others of the wonderful things you do."

Bio:

Over 45 years of marriage, raising three sons, volunteering in my community, church and schools has given me endless opportunities to see things as they could be and do the unusual and unexpected. I have two web sites to encourage Christians worldwide and published an eBook in 2012 "Encourage-Mints."

#16: The Cupbearer

By Laura J. Marshall

Like dirty fingerprints on a clear glass, so is the animosity that comes from someone in great opposition to God. The cup hovers over me, a reminder, as if the enemy whispers, "This one's mine." And I pray.

I am a cupbearer.

The smudged cups stack up. They cling to my mind in their emptiness.

Faith sees the potential.

Faith sees the need.

Faith sees the water that washes.

I am a cupbearer.

Sometimes I am afraid to see all the cups and carry them. Yet, I balance them in patience and gaze on them in forbearance and prayer.

I bear the cups to the feet of the Lord. He looks on them with compassion and love, tears filling His eyes, "It is for these I came into the world."

I can't help but spill a bit of the Lord's overflowing mercy as I walk.

I am a cupbearer.

I bear the cups with me as I go on my way. As my days increase, I carry more. Their weight can become heavy. Returning to His feet, I lift each one. He nods. Their burden becomes light. These I bear all my life with my life.

I am a cupbearer.

My prayers will be everlasting. For only God knows if a cup has been cleansed. I am just a cupbearer. I am not brave. Faith is brave. Valiant. Faith bears the cups.

Faith holds them close, closer still and looks on each with the ministrations of hope and confidence.

I am a cupbearer.

I am faith.

~~~~~~

Faith is active and has substance.

The longer I travel through this life, the more I collect faces of wrath, words, voices, gestures. Repeatedly they visit on the wings of the Holy Spirit. Some are more painful than others to look upon. Most didn't know I existed, but I saw, heard, or felt their presence. I've tried to protect my eyes and ears, weighing my steps and where I tread, yet our paths cross and I often wonder if it isn't divined by God. Through our faith, we all are cupbearers…carrying others in prayer to the feet of the Lord. Faith is modest, industrious, courageous, and confident. It has great influence. As I ponder the picture God gave me, I wonder why I wasn't carrying cups of wrath. The cups were empty, smudged and dirty. Do I carry the cups of my children to the feet of the Lord? Are they colorful and with fingerprints? Are they empty vessels or full?

Bio:

Laura J. Marshall is the full-time mother of five sons and part-time writer and blogger. She operates a popular blog called The Old Stone Wall. Laura writes devotionals and inspirational romantic suspense. A Mom's Battle Cry to Overcome Fear , the second book in her best-selling Battle Cry Devotional Series, has just released. Visit www.LauraJMarshall.com to find out more about Laura's books.

#17: Learning to Stand

By Cheryl Rogers

"The Lord shall fight for you, and ye shall hold your peace."
Exodus 14:14 KJV

Prayer is powerful.

When I succumbed to a severe immune disorder many years ago, I learned just how powerful. After seeking prayer wherever and whenever I could, God restored my life to me. But now He has brought me to a new place in my faith walk.

I had become accustomed to storming heaven with prayer requests for myself and my loved ones. I'd become accustomed to calling on the intercessors, praying and fasting when I could. Now God whispers: Hold your peace and watch Me work for you. I ask myself – Do I really need to try and convince Him? Am I praying for something He doesn't want too? Am I praying for something He has already done? Because I am praying the promises He has made in His Word, I know the answers.

We are spiritual creatures. What we see manifested in the flesh happens first in the spirit realm. So when I was healed many years ago, the healing initially occurred when the Holy Spirit came to indwell me. That was the real healing. I became a true child of God, gifted and called for His purposes on Earth. No longer alone, powerless against the enemy. No longer spiritually bruised and battered, because HE came into my life.

He also quickened my mortal body by His Spirit (Romans 8:11). It took a while for that to manifest in my body weakened by a disease doctors were powerless to defeat. But it wasn't too much for God, the One who made me and who knew how to fix me. It wasn't too much for the God that crafted our bodies fearfully and wonderfully (Psalm 139:14), enabling them to heal themselves if they are given the proper fuel and rest.

Through that experience, I learned to depend upon God, not man. I learned He's made our bodies resilient and with an incredible capacity for abuse. We're assaulted by toxins, food additives and stress. Our food is denatured and stripped of the nutrients God has placed there for us. We whip up concoctions that taste great but do little but add inches to our waistlines. In the end, we can't top what He's already given us.

I learned to rely on God for the answers to my questions and solutions to my problems. Although my natural inclination is to peruse the Internet for answers, at times I let Him quiet this urging. Deep inside, I know He already has the answers. Deep inside, I know He is with me and for me (Hebrews 13:5). And I know I can't trust myself to sort lies from truth.

And so, in this new place, I realize God is calling on me to trust Him, to recognize I must wait for His plan to unfold. Instead of letting panic reign, He has called me to a faith that does indeed move mountains rather than quake in fear.

The gentle whispering of the Holy Spirit comforts me, assuring me of His presence and of His faithfulness. He whispers that He desires to answer my prayers right now, but lets me know it's not the best plan.

He is showing me when we can't change others or our circumstances, we can still change ourselves.

And so I have a choice. I can focus on the good things, make the most of what I have, pray unceasingly for Him to make good on the promises in His word, and stand in faith. Or I can give in to self-pity, doubt and misery. I can focus on the problems and feel overwhelmed. I can give up.

I love prayer intercessors. I intercede for others. But in this new place, I recognize He is my all. He is my Alpha and Omega (Revelation 1:11). I can stand in faith.

I'm still praying. I know we need to pray unceasingly (1 Thessalonians 5:17). I know we must resist the enemy so he will flee (James 4:7). I know our weapons are spiritual, not carnal (2 Corinthians 10:4). But my yoke is easy (Matthew 11:30) because I'm not taking on the weight of that responsibility. He has made and He will bear (Isaiah 46:4).

He intercedes for me (Romans 8:26).

Bio:

Cheryl Rogers came to know Christ as an adult after succumbing to a severe immune disorder and surrendering her life to Him. A former newspaper reporter, she has dedicated herself to sharing the good news of Christ through her writing. She writes eBooks and publishes New Christian Books Online Magazine:
http://www.songsfromtheword.com/NewChristianBooks.

#18: A New Beginning

By Carol McCormick

I came into this world during a time when traditional family life and values were the norm, but grew up with the fads and the standards of the 60's and 70's.

During my teenage years, I didn't have much interest in spiritual things, other than an occasional prayer before bed. I often skipped religious instruction classes to go downtown and sit on the benches in front of city hall, to smoke cigarettes and watch boys go by. The Vietnam War was in full swing, as were student, political, prison, and race riots. The 70's brought a revolution, and with it, turbulence and a change in American culture and its values.

Enticed by the lure of pleasure, excitement, and the illusion of invincibility, I was caught up in a wave of rebellion, and engaged in many of the typical activities that were prevalent during the 70's hippie movement. Most of my friends were written up in the newspaper on a regular basis for breaking the law in one form or another, which led to my own lax attitude about authority.

When I turned eighteen, I moved out of the house and finished my last month of high school while living at friends' homes. Immediately after graduation, I began working as a hairstylist in a beauty salon where I found a loving family atmosphere that gave a sense of security and order to my life, although there was still something missing. A void existed in my heart that I could not fill with drinking, partying, or making money. I had no power to change my circumstances which were spiraling downhill fast, and I thought, is this all there is? There must be something more.

The following Christmas, I asked for and received a Bible as a gift. I opened it to the book of Genesis and read the Creation story, but I couldn't relate to anything there, so I turned to the New Testament and read the genealogies. I couldn't relate to anything there either, so I opened to the book of Proverbs where I found the seven things that the Lord hates. I could relate to some of those things, since I was doing them, so I closed the Bible, thinking that there was no hope for me and went further from the Lord for three more years.

Then one day while visiting my aunt, I found a book in her home about survival. Thinking it was about camping in the wilderness, I happily took it home. To my surprise, it was actually about the book of Revelation. The book opened up a whole new world to me that I had never heard about before. It said things like people would vanish in the "twinkling of an eye" and judgment would befall those left behind. I also noticed little words and numbers under these statements and somehow I knew they were Scriptures, so I looked them up. I was shocked to find that these strange quotes were really in the Bible, and I got scared. I knew that I would be in big trouble if these events occurred during my lifetime, so I started searching for answers.

It happened that around this time, my employer became a Christian. While working together, I asked her questions about her newfound faith, and after we had talked awhile, she said, "I know you're going to become a Christian, because you have the desire." But in my mind, I thought, "I wish it were true," but you really don't know me.

Shortly after this time, I heard a minister's wife speak about her rebellious past, and I suddenly felt there was hope for me in my own lost condition. As this woman described her wayward ways, I felt as though she was describing my life. When she quoted the Bible and said, "All have sinned and come short of the glory of God," and, "All we like sheep have gone astray, we have turned every one to his own way," I felt as though she was speaking to me. She said that Jesus bore all of our sins when He died on the cross and rose again, and then she proceeded to tell the audience that she was going to Heaven someday.

How could she say such a thing?!

I stayed behind to question this woman who made such a bold proclamation. I wanted to know, because deep in my heart, I wanted to go there too. She explained the way of salvation again in a sweet and loving tone, and I told her that I wanted to become a Christian, but I couldn't stop sinning. She showed me from the Bible that it is by grace that we are saved through faith, and that it was a gift from God. She asked me again if I would like to pray, and I said, "Not yet! I can't stop sinning!" I thought I had to be good first, before I came to Christ.

We went back-and-forth like this for three more times until she patiently showed me the verse that said, "Not by works of righteousness which we have done, but according to his mercy He saved us." I finally understood that God loved me right where I was and that Jesus died for all of my sins. I was ready to stop going my own way and surrender my life to Christ. She led me in a prayer that changed my life as I asked for forgiveness and asked Jesus to come into my heart and save me. At that moment, I felt clean inside. A huge burden seemed to have been lifted from my shoulders, and I had a new beginning. I was free! I was forgiven! And by the grace of God, I was going to Heaven!

Bio:

Carol has been a speaker for Christian Women's Connection (Stonecroft Ministries International) for over 15 years. She is also an international bestselling author who has appeared on regional and Christian television programs and has been a guest on over fifty Christian and secular radio stations. You can find out more about Carol McCormick and her books at... www.amazon.com/author/carolmccormick and http://www.carolmccormick.com.

#19: Faith Like a Mustard Seed

By Victor Brodt
Luke 17:1-10

"I have seen many cases like this before; she fits all the profiles." The doctor quickly spoke as he flashed various tests and charts before my gaze. The papers flew by too quickly for even the most trained eye. He was a busy person, most often the last in the line of experts. He seemed to carry the weight of a man hounded by the masses to fix what no one else could solve.

"She may have 6 months to live," the doctor pronounced pointedly.

There in the busy hospital hallway, a nurse's station buzzed and whirled, but for me time slowly froze and the noise faded. The walls grew close as if the whole world was shrinking. Life would get even harder. His quick, curt speech was supposed to prepare me to lose the love of my life.

I thought that I had already done one of the hardest things in life, I had left my pastorate. It was a wonderful growing church, the attendance had doubled in short order; it was my dream come true; interrupted by a nightmare. We found that I needed to leave behind my plans, my hopes, and my dreams in order to care for my beloved bride as she went through surgeries and mysterious afflictions.

There in the hospital hallway, I stared at the stark green walls; it seemed only moments before when my wife and I had gazed at another view; it was a time when we knew very little about things religious. We were on our honeymoon touring Europe. We took in all of the artwork we could; there was one stop on the highly recommended list, a church called Sacred Heart. There we stood looking up at something like the unfathomable expanse of the Grand Canyon, but this was man-made. The huge dome contained a ceramic mosaic designed to last to the end of time. It seemed to me a perfect artistry. The tiles made up the largest of paintings, and one subject surrounded you, and lovingly looked into your eyes. There he was, arms wide open; it was Jesus. We felt as if we had met him for the first time, as if we could now see His love. The artist had captured the impossible. Perhaps this would be exactly like our first glimpse of real heaven.

There in the hospital hallway, I wanted us to just be in His arms. I wished my wife and I could simply go to Him, now, together...

After Sacred Heart we continued our tour of Europe, but shortly we made a distinction. There were churches, and then there were Jesus churches; some were centered on relics and material things. Some were centered on Jesus, and seemed to exude His love and wonder. In a hotel in Florence, Italy, my beautiful bride, a Jewish lady, did, what we thought at the time, no one like her in 2000 years had done. She prayed to receive Jesus. The decision was not a casual or easy one for either of us.

When we returned to the US we were amazed to find others like us who had found the real Jesus. Life became unusual; together we were baptized in the ocean. On Malibu beach, a sunbathing Jane Fonda was an unwitting witness. Not long afterward we toured the world with an evangelistic group. My wife and I were firebrands, and we experienced what often seemed just like living chapters in the book of Acts. Surely God was with us. Then there was seminary, a son, and finally finding the place I felt I belonged even before I had become a Christian; the pastorate. Life was very good, and then suddenly came the nightmare.

The Wall of Pain

Pain demands your attention, severe pain may be numbed with drugs or other means, but when it refuses to relent it becomes unbearable. When hope fades, it gets even worse. We did not know the real future but the doctor was wrong; she lived and we struggled on. Many voices told us to give up. Often I told her I felt her pain; little did we realize that we actually shared the same affliction; hers was much further along, but I was busy doing the best I could to care for her.

When we were first married, we thought there could be no couple that could love each other more, but there really is much, much more to real love. The struggle taught us more than we could have imagined. When there is serious long term suffering it comes down to a decision, a decision to love, a decision to face the impossible, and a decision to forgive and resolve. There are many ways to cut and run, but Christian or not there is a kind of decision that really is faith being worked out.

I started a new business that was flexible for my wife's care and somehow with God's help we managed to be very successful; this allowed us to try every medical option imaginable but it is clear to me that it was really faith that held us together. Ultimately behind my story is a common secret that keeps many of us from utter ruin; it is our God given tendency to apply faith to even the most difficult of situations.

When it comes to the things of the Bible I am very well educated. I learned Greek and Hebrew. I studied under some of the best scholars. Truthfully faith is gigantic and beyond comprehension. I understand faith somewhat; but you should know that faith is a concept that humbles all mortals. We often fail and flail. Faith could feel weak, even when it may be very strong. If you think of faith like building a muscle you will get confused; you are not a 90 lb. weakling that just needs to try harder. It is a self-defeating lie to feel guilty because you have not exercised enough faith. It might be best to think of faith as a fragile gift, a gift you cannot buy from others, or earn. The gift awaits you but there are some things to understand, some things which hinder and some that help.

Faith is not ignoring reality and trying to believe something that is not true. It is not a pull yourself up by your boot straps attitude. In the Biblical sense it is not simply a positive attitude or the mindset that everything will go your way; this is really an old distorted view that comes from man and it is not God's manner.

Faith is increased by absorbing God's word so fully, that you listen and do what it says in spite of what other voices say. Faith is evidenced by applying God's principles. Biblical giving and serving will allow your faith to grow, but choosing to worry and fear will eat away at your soul and you will be misled into feeling like you have no faith at all. Unforgiveness and bitterness will most likely make your faith feel as powerless as Samson after a haircut. This should never be.

Over twenty-five years ago, the doctor gave my wife 6 months to live. I wonder if he is still alive? My wife is. Life has not been easy, nor has it gone as planned; in fact it has been an impossible journey. In the midst of all this, love, respect, and admiration have grown deep and enormously strong. Faith has somehow turned the pain into something precious like gold; eternal gold. We have often felt weak, but after all this time I also know there is something very strong; it is very much like a mustard seed, and it is also very much like a great and strong tree planted by deep waters.

Bio:

Victor Brodt - Author, Artist, and Speaker. He especially loves to tell stories about a famous old dog named Jack. They're parables and reflections of Jesus and God's love for you. Despite great challenges, Victor and his wife are encouragers and ministers to the core. Google his unique name.

#20: Releasing Divine Faith

By Rev. Paul B. Heidt

God made magnificent promises to each of us in his Word—the sixty-six books of the Bible. They are not dead words as so many people believe. No, they are alive as much now as ever before. How do you identify what God is saying to you through His Word and have enough faith to see it come to pass in your life? The steps for how to do that are clear when we see how the faith of a leader named Joshua worked to accomplish God's plan for his life.

God promised Joshua that he would lead the children of Israel into the Promised Land of Israel. That meant leading two million Hebrews over a flooded river, commanding thousands of soldiers to clear the land of its pagan beliefs and, ultimately, taking possession of its villages. Why did Joshua attempt such an enormous task? Perhaps the primary reason is that God gave him a promise that He would be with Joshua throughout the process, never leaving him or forsaking him, just as He was with Moses.

Foreseeing the obstacles and struggles that awaited him, it took Joshua great courage and great faith to take the reins of Moses and move God's children into their promised possession. Joshua's faith didn't rely on the tradition and rules given to Moses nor did Joshua sit back and make faith a god—expecting God's promise to come into being without any effort on his part. Joshua knew that he needed a divine faith that would bring him victory—a faith that is available to each of us.

Behind every great accomplishment for God is a great season of preparation. This was true for Joshua—God's leader and general over Israel who led two million plus Hebrews into their promised land. We get a hint of his preparation in Joshua 1:1:

"Now after the death of Moses, the servant of the Lord it came to pass that the Lord spoke to Joshua, the son of Nun, Moses' minister." (NKJV- emphasis mine).

The word "minister" is significant because it can also be translated "disciple," "servant," or "aid." I like the word "servant." This is a critical concept to grasp because genuine faith that prepares to possess God's promises always begins with servanthood. Joshua lived a servant life as he built his faith and pursued God's plan for his life, and so can you.

Possess a Servant's Heart

Have you felt called into the five-fold ministry—apostle, prophet, evangelist, pastor, or teacher? Or do you think you've been anointed to succeed as a business person, nurse, contractor, or other occupation? Whichever path God leads you into, it doesn't begin on the platform of a church or behind a desk in an executive suite. It begins by being somebody else's aid—following somebody else around, setting up chairs, washing someone's car and doing someone else's errands with a servant's attitude.

Why is being a servant such an important aspect of faith? It's simple. If you cannot obey and serve someone you can see, will you really be able to obey and serve God whom you cannot?

Rick Renner, a great Bible teacher and author, said that while he was preparing for ministry, a prominent pastor asked him to shine his alligator shoes. How would you have felt about that request? Grateful? Ready to shine? Rick did his duty, albeit grudgingly. Fortunately, he learned the principle of servanthood over time, and it has produced much fruit in his ministry today.

I remember a guest speaker who came to my church a long time ago. After a three-hour service wearing three-inch high heels, she and her disciple came to my house. The speaker sat on my sofa and took off her shoes. What do you think her aid did? Without even being asked, she walked up to the speaker and proceeded to massage her feet. I said to myself, now there's a servant!

Remember: a faith that won't willingly submit in serving others is a faith that won't be released to accomplish God's plan.

Some of the most important days in my ministry preparation involved learning how to submit to men and women of God in the church, at Bible College, and in seminary. I remember the night that no one wanted to help a well-known evangelist at his resource table during a conference at Zion Bible College. Everyone wanted to be in the service to see what God was doing, including me. Yet, something prompted me to help the evangelist in the exhibit hall. So I did. At the last second, he changed his mind and decided to set up his table in the gym where the service was in progress. I learned the importance of being a servant when no one else wanted to be, and I was rewarded for it. I received a double blessing: I enjoyed the service and was blessed to assist the man of God at his resource table.

Invariably, choosing to serve someone at your own expense is not easy. It doesn't always result in a blessing either, at least not right away. Nevertheless, if you want a faith that possesses God's plan for your life, it begins by being a servant now, a minister now, someone's aid now.

You might say, "I've never heard that serving others is a part of faith." That's why so few people actually walk by faith or manifest great faith! Too many people in the church would rather listen to messages about faith than release it through true servanthood. Paul discussed this problem in his letter to the Philippians:

"I trust in the Lord Jesus to send Timothy to you shortly, that I also may be encouraged when I know your state. For I have no one like-minded, who will sincerely care for your state. For all seek their own, not the things which are of Christ Jesus. But you know his proven character, that as a son with his father he served with me in the gospel." (Philippians 2:19-22, NKJV-emphasis mine).

Timothy served Paul. Paul served Barnabas. The disciples served Christ. Elisha served Elijah. And Joshua served Moses. Serving others is an important dynamic of releasing divine faith. It prepares you for possessing God's plan, and you will never possess it without grasping how faith works through servanthood.

Bio:

Rev. Paul B. Heidt
Lead Pastor of Living Hope Assembly of God
Hamlin, New York

#21: When Motives Are Rewarded

By Marilynn Dawson

My faith story seems to be a never-ending series of adventures. I entered another one at the end of January 2013.

That day, my boss sat me down in his office and nearly broke into tears twice as he shared that due to lack of work he'd have to let me go. The news hurt, but he was the one needing a hug when it was over. He is a fellow believer and attends a local Mennonite church with his family.

That night I was tempted to get concerned about the future, 'til I realized God had just answered my prayer for time to make two changes in my current lifestyle. One change was to add time for walks. Walking is my favorite form of exercise and I haven't been able to do it as much as I used to. The other was to regain uninterrupted quiet time with just me and the unseen Lover of my soul. Sure it's good to have conversational prayer off and on throughout the day, to open the Scriptures to answer someone. But I wanted that quiet private time too. As a single working mother, that isn't an easy thing to schedule on a regular basis due to life changing every 3 to 6 months whether I need it to or not. So there I was that evening, realizing that suddenly I could call my own hours again! I could put these two desires into action finally!

I began my quiet times reviewing a devotional on Genesis by Nicole Vaughn. The first week I had two days of self-employed work. I had devotions every morning and only missed one day's walk. The second week there was hardly any self-employed work, but again, only really missed one day's walk. Then February 18th arrived!

A realtor my former boss knows from the local Rotary club called wanting to hire someone, as work for him is getting busy and he needed assistance in the office. He asked if I'd come for an interview at 7pm that night. I'm not really sold on the idea of secretarial work, but as it was a referral from my former boss, I couldn't say no and went for what would be a very casual, unstructured, "help me while we talk" interview that I got paid for! I assisted him for two hours as we talked about what I was expecting, the wage, the hours I was hoping to engage in to implement desired changes in my life, etc. This realtor accommodated without much hassle.

Friday of that week, employment paperwork was signed at my asking wage, with the desired hours!

This is only part-time work 3 days a week until work picks up, then possibly a full workweek. . . The offered income is before deductions, so take-home will be less than what I need (which is far less than most people are used to in our culture). But this whole thing smacks of God showing pleasure in my excitement that I could spend alone time with Him again; granting me a form of work that wasn't my first choice, but that promises adventure all on its own.

My application for Canada's Employment Insurance has the potential to be cancelled almost before it starts.

Christ says in Matthew 6:33 (KJV), "But seek ye first the kingdom of God, and his righteousness; and all these things shall be added unto you."

The focus is not to be on things we need, nor should our focus in seeking God be our needs. Our "me first" culture in the Church teaches that if you want your needs met, focus on God - basically saying that our motive to focus on God is so that our needs will be met. To the contrary, we should be focusing on God whether or NOT our needs are EVER met! Our motive is precisely because God is worthy of that focus. God has already done all He ever needs to do to earn our love and devotion by rescuing us from sin via His Son, Jesus Christ. It is when we take our eyes off our needs and put them onto God that God is freed to move on our behalf in whatever capacity He deems best. Our attitude should be that of Job's who said, "Though He slay me, yet will I praise Him" (see Job 13:15). God isn't required to meet our needs just because we feign to put Him first. God isn't a genie who, when rubbed the right way, gives us all that our hearts desire. Instead, the Scriptures say when we get close to God's heart, He will plant desires within us. (See Psalm 37:4)

I lost my day job when the economic climate of my city was depressed. Yet I was excited for the chance to spend time in God's presence. There has been a sense of excitement and adventure ever since. I didn't know what was going to happen or when, but it's happening and I'm tightening my seatbelt because I have no idea where this ride will stop next.

God can't help showing up when we draw near. He did promise that when we draw near to Him, He would draw near to us (see James 4:8). He can't resist those who choose to spend time with Him just for Who He is. We all want to be accepted and loved for who we are, not for what we look like or what we can do. We were formed in God's image. He feels that way too. He shows up every time we choose to love Him for being Him - No "I'm doing this so God will do that", just spending time with God for who He is.

80

God didn't have to bring that job along. I don't even know if this job is my final destination at this point on the journey. All I know is that God chose to honor my desire to give Him private time.

Bio:

Marilynn lives with her two teenagers, cat and gerbil, in Canada. In the evenings and on weekends she's a sound tech doing various events through the year from funerals to workshops to concerts and weddings. Marilynn sings in the choir and sang on her church's praise teams for several years.

Conclusion

By Shelley Hitz

There you have it! 21 stories of faith. I also encourage you to read Hebrews 11 where many other stories of faith are listed. And I'm sure you also have stories of your own to share. I know I do.

In closing, I want to share two specific instances where God taught me about stepping out in faith. These include two major geographical moves where my faith was tested.

The first move, was in 2002 when we packed all of our earthly belongings into a 1988 Suburban and drove it to Belize, Central America. We ended up living there as short-term missionaries for two years. It was definitely a step of faith to quit both of our jobs, sell most of our stuff and move to a foreign country. However, on top of all of that, the Ayala's, the missionaries that would be our main contact in Belize, told us that there were currently no rental properties available for us to live in when we arrived. Therefore, we would have to live in a hotel until something opened up.

I have to admit that I didn't demonstrate the perfect picture of faith during our drive down to Belize. However, I am so thankful that God is patient with us and willing to teach us along the way. Aren't you?

Instead of trusting God to provide housing for us, I worried. Where were we going live? How long would we have to stay in a hotel? Would we have the finances necessary to stay in a hotel until a rental opened up? And the questions went on and on.

We had several delays along the way to Belize including a flat tire and other issues. So when we were finally getting ready to cross over into the Belize border, we called the Ayala's. We let them know that we would be arriving in Belize the next day. And to our surprise, they told us that a house came open that very day for us to rent. They would be able to provide bedding and a few groceries for us so that we could even spend that very first night in our new house. We did not even have to spend one night in a hotel. Amazing!

However, 10 years later, we had another major move. This time we were moving to Colorado Springs, Colorado. We did not have the money at the time to fly out in advance to find a place to rent. Therefore, we did a lot of research online. Being a planner, I wanted to have a place ready to move into when we arrived in Colorado. However, my husband, CJ, wanted to actually see the place first before we signed a contract. Looking back, I am so thankful that he insisted we do it this way. But at the time, once again, I allowed worry to creep into my mind instead of trusting God to provide.

We packed all of our stuff into the moving truck and arrived in Colorado Springs on a Friday night. We needed to return the moving truck by Tuesday morning, so we had a few days to find a place to move in to or we would need to move our stuff into a storage unit in the meantime. Thankfully, a couple of realtors were willing to show us rentals over the weekend. On Sunday we visited a condo that was within our price range, in the area we wanted to live and we decided to apply to rent there. We told them our timeframe and unbelievably they were able to meet with us the next day to sign the paperwork, give us the keys and allow us to start moving in to our new place. We were completely moved in by late Monday night and were able to return the moving truck Tuesday morning and not even have to pay a late fee. Once again, God provided in an amazing way that increased my faith.

One of my heroes of the faith, Corrie ten Boom, said "Faith is like radar that sees through the fog -- the reality of things at a distance that the human eye cannot see."

How true that is! We are all on a faith journey of our own. Each day we can choose to either walk by faith or walk by sight. My prayer for myself and for you is that we learn to walk by faith.

Let me close with a prayer...

Lord, we thank You today that You are the author and perfecter of our faith. Thank You for Your patience with us on this faith journey. Empower us to keep our eyes fixed on You, Jesus, as we walk through the circumstances of life each day. Strengthen our faith in You today. We love You and praise You. In Jesus's name we pray, Amen.

Get Free Christian Books

Love getting FREE Christian books online? If so, sign up to get notified of new Christian book promotions and never miss out. Then, grab a cup of coffee and enjoy reading the free Christian books you download.

You will also get our FREE report, *"How to Find Free Christian Books Online"* that shows you 9 places you can get new books…for free!

Sign up at:
www.bodyandsoulpublishing.com/freebooks

Happy reading!

Contact Information:

We would love to hear from you! Send us an e-mail to the following addresses:

cj@cjhitz.com
shelley@shelleyhitz.com

Websites:
www.bodyandsoulpublishing.com
www.christianspeakers.tv

Fixing our eyes on Jesus,
CJ & Shelley Hitz

CJ and Shelley Hitz

C.J. and Shelley Hitz enjoy sharing God's Truth through their speaking engagements and their writing. On downtime, they enjoy spending time outdoors running, hiking and exploring God's beautiful creation.

To find out more about their ministry check out their website at www.BodyandSoulPublishing.com or to invite them to your next event go to www.ChristianSpeakers.tv.

Note from the Author: Reviews are gold to authors! If you have enjoyed this book, would you consider reviewing it on Amazon.com? Thank you!

Other Books by Shelley Hitz

A Life of Faith

A Life of Gratitude

Trusting God When Bad Things Happen

Finding Hope in the Midst of Tragedy

Forgiveness Formula

Unshackled and Free

Mirror Mirror… Am I Beautiful?

Teen Devotionals… for Girls!

See the entire list at: www.ShelleyHitz.com

www.ingramcontent.com/pod-product-compliance
Lightning Source LLC
Chambersburg PA
CBHW071906020426
42331CB00010B/2696